Prayer Pals
21-DAY Challenge

For Women of Faith

KRISTIN OVERSTREET

WESTBOW
PRESS®
A DIVISION OF THOMAS NELSON
& ZONDERVAN

WestBow Press books may be ordered through booksellers or by contacting:

WestBow Press
A Division of Thomas Nelson & Zondervan
1663 Liberty Drive
Bloomington, IN 47403
www.westbowpress.com
1 (866) 928-1240

ISBN: 978-1-9736-4662-4 (sc)
ISBN: 978-1-9736-4663-1 (e)

Library of Congress Control Number: 2018913987

Print information available on the last page.

WestBow Press rev. date: 12/07/2018

Then he continued, "Do not be afraid, Daniel. Since the first day that you set your mind to gain understanding and to humble yourself before your God, your words were heard, and I have come in response to them.
Daniel 10:12

Contents

A Word from the Author

I want to take this opportunity to thank my Lord and Savior Jesus Christ, who has been the director of this challenge from the beginning, using my mind, body, and spirit to achieve His purpose. This challenge is very personal and dear to me, as it is based on my testimony of praying with a co-worker, Angela Blankenship, throughout two years. During that time, Angela and I saw God work in our lives in miraculous ways. As a result, I was compelled by God to share this praying technique with other believers.

Although the name of this program, "Prayer Pals 21-Day Challenge," indicates that you will be praying with a pal for 21 days, it is more than that! As women of faith come together and pray persistently three times a day for 21 days something powerful happens! It no longer becomes a "you prayer" but an "us prayer." In other words, you and your prayer pal will experience the closeness of sisterly love as you are listening, encouraging and praying for one another's needs–all while drawing closer to God–together! The Prayer Pals 21 Day Challenge book allows you and your prayer pal to stay focused each day, and learn from one of the greatest prayer warriors in the Bible–Daniel!

My hope for you is that after completing this challenge, you will be stronger in Christ, gain a prayer pal for life and gain a closer walk with Christ.

May God Bless You,

Kristin Overstreet

The Layout of This Book

Prayer Pals 21-Day Challenge book has three sections: pre-challenge, challenge, and post-challenge.

Pre-Challenge	**Challenge**	**Post Challenge**
This section provides step-by-step instructions on how to set up your 21-day challenge including information on:	The Challenge section provides you with what to do during the 21-day challenge including:	The Post challenge provides you with what to do after your challenge ends which includes:
Selecting a pal	Daily scriptures from the book of Daniel Chapter 6 and 10.	Celebrating the completion of your 21-Day Challenge with your pal
Creating a prayer list	A reflection of the scriptures that take a more in-depth look at one of the greatest prayer warriors in the Bible—Daniel!	Continuing prayers for 21 additional days using the Prayer Pals 21-Day Challenge Continuation Journal
Developing a plan to pray		
Being accountable and committed to the challenge	A daily journal with self-reflection questions that examine your mind, body, and spirit.	Becoming a Prayer Pals 21-Day Challenge Leader at your church or in your community.
Keeping focus-by learning the four Principles of Prayer Pals 21-Day Challenge	An optional social media challenge	
	Prayer Focus	
	Prayer Tracker	

How Does the 21-Day Challenge Program Work?

The Prayer Pals 21-Day Challenge program consists of praying with a pal three times a day for 21 days utilizing the Prayer Pals 21-Day Challenge Book. Each section of this book is specifically designed to support prayer pal challengers before, during and after the challenge is complete.

I. Pre-Challenge Section

In this section, you will follow the step-by-step instructions and select your prayer pal. This person can be any person of faith including your mother, daughter, friend, sister, aunt, grandmother, or another relative. Once a prayer pal is selected, challengers will follow the step-by-step instructions in their Prayer Pals 21-Day Challenge book. It is also strongly encouraged for challengers to read Daniel Chapter 6 before beginning the 21-day challenge.

II. Challenge Section

The challenge not only consists of praying with someone three times a day for 21 days, but it also involves interacting in your Prayer Pals 21-Day Challenge Book. So as you progress through each day of the challenge, you will have a specific scripture to reflect and focus on for the day. As you reflect, you will be asked to self-examine your mind, body, and spirit and think about how you can discipline yourself to pray more like Daniel. As you pray with your prayer pal three times a day, it is encouraged to share with your prayer pal your journal entries. Although this may be uncomfortable to some, this act of vulnerability allows you to confess your faults one to another, encourage each other and be more devoted to your prayers. In addition to scriptures and reflections, you will find social media challenges throughout the 21 days so that you can apply what you have learned. At the end of the day be sure to bubble in your prayer progress and update your prayer needs list.

III. Post-Challenge

After the 21 days has ended, you are encouraged to share out your Prayer Pals 21-Day Challenge testimony at your church, through social media, or with a friend, co-worker, or a family member. If you are inspired to share this challenge with others from your church or community, then consider being a Prayer Pals 21-Day Challenge Group Leader. As a Prayer Pals leader, you will have the opportunity to start your own Prayer Pals group at your church or organization. If you are inspired to keep praying with your prayer pal, utilize the 21 additional days of prayer journaling found on page 73.

How Do I Pray?

In Matthew 6:9-13 we read of Jesus teaching his disciples how they should pray. This popular Scripture is known as The Lord's Prayer and is our greatest example as Christians as to how we should pray.

"This, then, is how you should pray:
"'Our Father in heaven,
hallowed be your name,
your kingdom come,
your will be done,
on earth as it is in heaven.
Give us today our daily bread.
And forgive us our debts,
as we also have forgiven our debtors.
And lead us not into temptation,
but deliver us from the evil one.

What can we learn from The Lord's Prayer? God desires our praise, wants to know our needs, and wants us to keep our heart clean and pure.

The ACTS model is helpful as you learn how to pray. ACTS stands for Adoration, Confession, Thanksgiving, and Supplication. It is as follows:

- Adoration means worship; praising God for who He is and for all that He has done for you. Most prayers begin with some form of adoration to God.
- Confession means admitting to God about the things you have said, thought, or done that is not pleasing to Him. When you confess your sins, you receive God's cleansing, and this helps to remove any barrier in your communication with Him.
- Thanksgiving means thanking God for your blessings.
- Supplication means praying for your needs and the needs of others.

Keep in mind that the ACTS model serves as a guide to help you pray, not as a rigid formula to follow. Your prayers should be in a natural and simple language that you are comfortable speaking. Remember, God already knows everything about you, so feel free to be who you are when you pray.

How Do I Pray With a Pal?

Before praying, make sure you are in an environment that is free from distraction, noise or other possible interferences. Take time to reflect on each of your prayer needs and daily journal entries.

Once you are in a quiet place, one person will lead the prayer aloud. It is recommended that you and your pal take turns praying aloud. This means person 1 will lead the morning prayer, person 2 will lead the mid-day prayer, and then person 1 will lead the evening prayer. If one person does not feel comfortable praying aloud, then the person that is comfortable will lead all the prayers.

During your prayer it is important to talk to God on behalf of yourself and your prayer pal, making mention of both prayer needs. Here is an example of how prayer might be expressed to cover both of your needs:

> Dear Heavenly Father,
>
> We want to **praise** you for this day! We **thank** you for bringing us together and for the salvation that we have through you. Father, we ask that you **forgive** us of any sin or wrongdoing that might hinder this prayer from reaching your throne of grace. We ask that you help keep us on the path of righteousness. God, we bring our **petitions** (tell God your prayer needs) to you, trusting that if it is **your will** that you will deliver us. We **thank** you again, Father, for what you have done for us, and we give all of these needs to you in your son Jesus name, Amen!

Prayer time is thought to be an intimate time between your pal, God, and yourself. Every prayer should be natural and from the heart. Don't worry about how your prayer will sound aloud to your prayer pal. Some people find it easier to put their pal on speaker phone so that they can pray in a position that feels more natural when talking to God.

Prayer Pals 21-Day Challenge

PRE-CHALLENGE SECTION

Step 1: Select an "Alliance"

Scripture

Two are better than one,
>   because they have a good return for their labor:
[10] If either of them falls down,
>   one can help the other up.
But pity anyone who falls
>   and has no one to help them up.
[11] Also, if two lie down together, they will keep warm.
>   But how can one keep warm alone?
[12] Though one may be overpowered,
>   two can defend themselves.
A cord of three strands is not quickly broken.—Ecclesiastes 4:9-12

Reflection

There is so much power when God's people come together! This scripture lets us know that "two are better than one," and are stronger together. The first step of this challenge is to select a prayer pal. Your prayer pal should be a woman of faith that is 100% committed to praying with you, three times a day for 21 days. It is essential that you take time to pray for God's guidance in helping you select the best prayer pal for you. As you pray about who your prayer pal will be, take time to consider the following things: 1. Will your prayer pal be committed to praying with you for 21 days, three times a day? 2. Does your prayer pal believe in the power of prayer? 3. Will your prayer pal hold you accountable to pray, and encourage you when you don't feel like praying?

Pray

As you begin to think about who to select for a prayer pal, it is important that you take time to pray and reflect. Is there someone in your life that you always go to when you need prayer or is there someone in your life that you consider a strong prayer warrior? Today, ask God to help guide your decision for a prayer pal.

All About My Prayer Pal

My prayer pal is:

My relationship to my prayer pal is:

My prayer pal is special to me because:

My prayer pal is special to me because:

My prayer pal's greatest strengths are:

My prayer pal's favorite bible verse is:

What does your prayer pal hope to gain from this challenge?

Step 2: Discuss "Your Needs" with Your Prayer Pal

Scripture

Do not be anxious about anything, but in every situation, by prayer and petition, with thanksgiving, present your requests to God.—Philippians 4:6

Reflection

This scripture instructs us to not worry about anything and to pray about everything. It also instructs us to give thanks to God and present your requests to Him. So as you get ready to begin your challenge, think about things in your life that you want to focus on during the next 21 days. Maybe it is a job change, or family problem, or health issue; whatever the needs are list them on your prayer needs list on the following page.

Journal

In your journal, you will select the three prayer needs to focus on during the 21-day challenge. Although you may have more than three prayer needs, it is essential that you focus on the things that are most important to you. Your prayer pal will also come up with three prayer needs to focus on during this challenge. You will write your prayer pal's prayer needs in your journal.

Pray

The goal is to make your prayers very specific and focus on the things that matter to you most. After you make a list of your prayer needs, take a few minutes and pray—letting those needs be made known to God. The night before you begin your 21-day challenge, you and your prayer pal will discuss each of your prayer needs. This page will constantly be reflected upon during the challenge and as prayers are answered.

My Prayer Needs

Prayer Needs	Progress	Important Dates
1.		
2.		
3.		

My Prayer Pal's Prayer Needs

Prayer Needs	Progress	Important Dates
1.		
2.		
3.		

Step 3: Prayer "Routine" of "Persistency"

Scripture

Then Jesus told his disciples a parable to show them that they should always pray and not give up. He said: "In a certain town there was a judge who neither feared God nor cared what people thought. And there was a widow in that town who kept coming to him with the plea, 'Grant me justice against my adversary.'

"For some time he refused. But finally he said to himself, 'Even though I don't fear God or care what people think, yet because this widow keeps bothering me, I will see that she gets justice, so that she won't eventually come and attack me!'"

And the Lord said, "Listen to what the unjust judge says. And will not God bring about justice for his chosen ones, who cry out to him day and night? Will he keep putting them off? I tell you, he will see that they get justice, and quickly. However, when the Son of Man comes, will he find faith on the earth?"—Luke 18:1-8

Reflection

In the scriptures above, Jesus tells the story of a widow that persistently bothered a judge with her pleas until he granted her justice. This parable teaches us the importance of praying persistently, and not losing heart. Although it may appear that God does not hear your prayers, it is important not to give up! For the next 21 days, you and your prayer pal will pray to God three times a day. This "routine" of "persistency" will soon become a natural part of your day.

Complete the following questions with your prayer pal.

First Day of 21-Day Challenge will begin on:

Last Day of 21-Day Challenge will end on:

We have agreed to pray together at these times every day:

How will you pray–by phone, in person or both?

Prayer Pals 21-Day Challenge

Accountability

Every challenge has a way to be accountable, right? Here are some ways to stay connected to the Prayer Pals 21-Day Challenge community.

1. **Connect**

Connect with a community of Prayer Pal 21-Day Challengers. Post pictures, ask questions and share your testimony of how this challenge is changing your life. Use the following link to connect to Prayer Pals 21-Day Challenge Group at: https://www.facebook.com/groups/139116480005729/?ref=bookmarks

Also be sure to like and follow Prayer Pals 21-Day Facebook Page at: https://www.facebook.com/prayerpals21days.

2. **Announce that your challenge is beginning**

The day before you start your challenge, it is encouraged that you post on the Prayer Pals 21 Facebook page a picture of you and your prayer pal together with the hashtag: #prayerpals21daychallenge. Be sure to say that you and your pal are "all in" this challenge.

3. **Private groups**

If you are completing this challenge within a group (church or other organization) it is recommended that you create a private group on social media to stay connected during this challenge. Private groups encourage challengers and help them keep focus.

4. **Completion of challenge**

After you complete your challenge, Prayer Pals 21-Day Challenge would love to hear from you! To show that you have completed your challenge it is encouraged that you and your pal take a picture holding your Prayer Pals 21-Day Challenge Certificate and post it on the Prayer Pals 21-Day Challenge, Facebook Page. If you are completing this challenge in a group setting, be sure to post pictures on the Prayer Pals 21-Day Challenge Facebook Page of your group and celebration. Use the hashtag: #prayerpals4life.

Keep Your Focus

Prayer Pals 21-Day Challenge
Four Essential Principles

To help you keep your focus during this challenge, use this acrostic to better understand the four essential principles of Prayer Pals 21-Day Challenge.

P. represents "persistency." Think about it like this, as you and your prayer pal come together to pray, your prayer needs are brought before God three times a day for 21 days!

R. represents "routine," forming a relationship with God as you pray each day three times a day. Getting into a habit of praying even when you are tired, hopeless, or just too busy. Praying with your pal will eventually become a natural part of your day, and you have gained a praying pal for life!

A. Represents "alliance," having a partner to share your burdens and pray with you. There is power in numbers!

Y. Represents "your needs" poured out to God. Things that have hindered you from growing, things that you gave up on praying about or any other need—give them to God and pray persistently.

21-Day Challenge Guide Tips

- ❖ **Pray Like Daniel!** The challenge is designed to pray with your prayer pal three times per day for 21 days. It is encouraged to pray like Daniel did, morning, noon and night.

- ❖ **Stay about the Father's business!** It is so easy when you get on the phone with your prayer pal to get sidetracked. It is okay to talk but don't forget to pray!

- ❖ **Can I pray with someone that is not a Christian?** Yes, in this case, the believer will lead the prayers. One of the prayer needs of the unbeliever may be for salvation. So this will be a perfect opportunity for the believer to witness the gospel to the unbeliever!

- ❖ **What if my prayer pal won't pray aloud?** The goal is for each person to build up the confidence to pray aloud. However in situations where your prayer pal is not comfortable in praying aloud, then you will assume the role of leading every prayer. It is essential to encourage your prayer pal to pray along with you during each prayer.

- ❖ **Why must we reflect during this journey?** Take time to talk with your prayer pal and encourage each other each day of the challenge. Discuss your journal entries as you feel comfortable. A significant part of this challenge is reflecting about what God is doing through you during the 21 days.

- ❖ **What if I miss a prayer?** You can easily make it up during the next prayer. In this situation, you will say two prayers on one phone call (each person will pray).

- ❖ **What if my prayer pal is unable to complete the challenge?** Sometimes life throws us curve balls and people have to quit the challenge. One solution to this problem is to try to find another prayer pal to step in and substitute. Another option is to stop and restart at a later time.

- ❖ **Yes, No or Growing?** These three things are the answers to your prayers. Throughout this challenge, you will likely be praying for a response from God. Reflect daily in your journal as to what God is saying to you.

- ❖ **21 days and then what?** That is up to you and your prayer pal to decide. You can keep on praying for an answer, or you can choose to stop.

Prayer Pals 21-Day Challenge

CHALLENGE SECTION

Day 1: Are Your Mind, Body, and Spirit in Sync?

Scripture

"In those days, I Daniel was mourning three full weeks. I ate no pleasant bread, neither came flesh nor wine in my mouth, neither did I anoint myself at all, till three whole weeks were fulfilled."—Daniel 10:2–3

Reflection

In these scriptures, it is evident that Daniel found himself in a place where he understood that he needed to remove anything in his life that would hinder his prayers from reaching the throne of God. Today, as you begin your prayer challenge, ask yourself this question, "Are you ready to get serious with God?" Is your prayer needs so important that you are willing to go the extra mile and pray with someone three times a day for 21 days? Are you able to remove anything from your life that might interfere with your prayer life? If so, you are in the mindset of Daniel, and you are ready to begin this challenge!

Journal

In your prayer journal today you will evaluate whether or not your mind, body, and spirit are in sync. As you self-reflect, think about each of these parts carefully. Are your thoughts positive and hopeful; meditating on the word of God, or do they tend to be cynical and doubtful about life and in constant worry or fear? How about your body? Is your body on the move for the Lord? Are you witnessing, serving others, and praising God through your words or deeds, or is your body busy with other things that are not of God? What about your spirit? How is your relationship with God? Are you talking to Him daily through prayer, or have you gotten too busy to pray and now feel cold or distant from God? Today, you will complete a pre-challenge evaluation of your mind, body, and spirit. You will complete this evaluation again at the midpoint, and at the conclusion of your challenge.

Optional Social Media Challenge

The day you gave your life to Christ was a perfect example when your mind, body, and spirit was in perfect sync! Your social media challenge for today is to find a picture of your baptism and post it on your social media. Make this your hashtag #mindbodyspiritinsync.

Prayer Journal Entry 1: Mind, Body, and Spirit Initial Questionnaire

Mind

Do you read your bible daily?	Yes	No
Do you spend time talking to God each day?	Yes	No
Do you meditate on the scripture each day?	Yes	No
Do you worry, fear or doubt about things in your life?	Yes	No

Body

Do you use your talents to serve God in some way?	Yes	No
Do you witness the gospel to others each day?	Yes	No
Do you praise God throughout your day?	Yes	No
Do you present your body as a living sacrifice for Christ?	Yes	No

Spirit

Do you feel close to God?	Yes	No
Do you keep the commandments?	Yes	No

What areas do you feel that you need growth in?

1.

2.

3.

Pray

As you and your prayer pal pray, take time to discuss today's journal entry with each other. Examine areas in each of your lives that need more growth, and pray for one another's mind, body and spiritual needs.

○ Prayer 1
○ Prayer 2
○ Prayer 3

Day 2: How Do Others See Me?

Scripture

It pleased Darius to appoint 120 satraps to rule throughout the kingdom, with three administrators over them, one of whom was Daniel. The satraps were made accountable to them so that the king might not suffer loss. Now Daniel so distinguished Himself among the administrators and the satraps by his exceptional qualities that the king planned to set Him over the whole kingdom.—Daniel 6:1–3

Reflection

King Darius appointed Daniel to become one of the three governors over 120 provinces. Due to the "excellent spirit" that was in him King Darius even gave it thought to let Daniel be over the whole kingdom! What a reputation and an impression that Daniel must have had on the King to entrust him with his kingdom! Even more so, when Daniel's co-workers became jealous of him, they too could not find any fault or error in him which was a testament as to what kind of man of God he was!

Journal

As you journal today, take some time to reflect on your reputation and the impression that you leave on the people around you. Ask yourself these questions: "How do others see me?" and "Do they know I am a Christian by my actions and words?" Proverbs 22:1 says: A good name is rather to be chosen than great riches, and loving favour rather than silver and gold. In your prayer journal today, list five words that describe you. After you list five words that describe you, think about how you use these attributes in the world around you and answer this question: "Do you use your attributes in a way that exemplifies Christ or do you use them in a way that does not allow others to see Christ through you?" Write your response in your journal.

Optional Social Media Challenge

As an extra, take time to poll your friends on social media by asking them to describe you in one word. See what attributes others use to describe you! Make this your hashtag: #howdoothersseeme?

Prayer Journal Entry 2: How Do Others See Me?

Five Words That Describe Me:

1.

2.

3.

4.

5.

Words That Others Use to Describe Me:

1.

2.

3.

4.

5.

Look at the two lists above. Do others see you the way that you see yourself? What surprised you the most from the list of how others see you?

Think about your qualities from the lists above. Do you use them in a way that exemplifies Christ? If so, how? If not, how can you begin to use them for Christ?

Pray

Today take time to discuss the attributes that you and your prayer pal wrote about in your journal. After you explain what you wrote, tell your prayer pal the qualities that you admire most about them. You may be surprised at what others think about you as often we are our own worst critic.

○ Prayer 1
○ Prayer 2
○ Prayer 3

Day 3: What Are My Faults?

Scripture

At this, the administrators and the satraps tried to find grounds for charges against Daniel in his conduct of government affairs, but they were unable to do so. They could find no corruption in Him, because he was trustworthy and neither corrupt nor negligent.—Daniel 6:4

Reflection

What an outstanding reputation that Daniel must have had for the people that worked alongside Him every day to have not found any fault or errors about him. Daniel was a model servant to his earthly king as well as his heavenly King. Today as you began to take a closer look at yourself, ask yourself this question: "What are my faults that I want to improve about myself?"

Journal

As you self-reflect, describe in your journal any faults that you may have. Determine ways that you can avoid putting yourself into situations where others may call you a hypocrite. The goal is to be like Daniel and keep a faithful and errorless reputation valued by the people around you.

Optional Social Media Challenge

As you scroll through social media, it is so easy to judge the post of others quickly; from their outward appearance to their successes, to their failures and the list goes on and on. So today you are going to do the opposite of what you typically do when you scroll through social media. So that means if you ignore certain people's posts; you will take time to comment something positive. The idea is to reach out to other people that you usually would not have. You can also privately message people that you have not spoken to in a while and give them some kind words.

Prayer Journal Entry 3: What Are My Faults?

What are some of the things that I would like to improve about myself?

What are some ways that I can work towards improving these things about myself?

What hinders me from improving these things about myself?

Pray

James 5:16 says, "Confess your faults one to another, and pray one for another, that ye may be healed. The effectual fervent prayer of a righteous man availeth much." Today you will confess your faults to your prayer pal, and as you pray for your prayer needs, you will also pray to be healed of your faults.

    ○ Prayer 1
    ○ Prayer 2
    ○ Prayer 3

Day 4: Are You in a Trap?

Scripture

Finally these men said, "We will never find any basis for charges against this man Daniel unless it has something to do with the law of his God.—Daniel 6:5

Reflection

The presidents and princes that worked alongside Daniel could not find any wrongdoings in him. However, they were jealous of Daniel, and they wanted nothing more than to see him fail. The officers knew that the only way to get Daniel in trouble was to create a trap that would possibly cause Daniel to fall. Today, the devil does an excellent job of creating traps all around us. He wants nothing more than to steal, kill and destroy all that God has given us. You may be in this situation right now where there are traps all around you, and you feel that there is no way out. 1 Peter 5:8 reminds us to "be alert and of sober mind because our enemy the devil prowls around like a roaring lion looking for someone to devour."

Journal

Today and in the days to come you and your prayer pal must be watchful for Satan's traps! Write down scriptures in your journal and share it with your payer pal on ways to be vigilant and to resist Satan's traps!

Optional Social Media Challenge

Share your scripture that you wrote in your journal with your friends on social media. Make this your hashtag: #bewatchfulandresist

Prayer Journal Entry 4: Are You in a Trap?

Write down at least two scriptures that remind you to be watchful of the devil.

Describe how you defend yourself against the devil and protect yourself from being caught in a trap.

Pray

Today as you pray, ask God to remove the "traps" that Satan puts in front of you and your prayer pal. Share with your prayer pal your scripture and an example of a time in your life when you were able to recognize Satan's trap and defended yourself from Him.

        ○ Prayer 1
        ○ Prayer 2
        ○ Prayer 3

Day 5: If God is for Us Who Can Be against Us?

Scripture

So these administrators and satraps went as a group to the king and said: "May King Darius live forever! The royal administrators, prefects, satraps, advisers, and governors have all agreed that the king should issue an edict and enforce the decree that anyone who prays to any god or human being during the next thirty days, except to you, Your Majesty, shall be thrown into the lions› den. Now, Your Majesty, issue the decree and put it in writing so that it cannot be altered—in accordance with the law of the Medes and Persians, which cannot be repealed." So King Darius put the decree in writing.—Daniel 6:6-9

Reflection

Take a minute to think about the number of people that conspired against Daniel. Scripture indicates that all of the government officials were involved in this plot to get rid of Daniel. Romans 8:31 says, "What, then, shall we say in response to these things? If God is for us, who can be against us?" Although Daniel's conspirers were numerous, Daniel had a much higher force on his side–His God!

Journal

Today as you think about your life and the people in this world that use you, discourage you, persecute you or make life difficult for you remember Daniel's story. He was the victim of the most extreme form of hate–murder! In your journal, think about a time that others conspired against you, and ultimately through your faith, God came to your rescue. Discuss what you did and how you were able to get through this challenging time.

Optional Social Media Challenge

Post Romans 8:31 on your social media today and make this your hashtag: #GodisForus.

Prayer Journal Entry 5: If God is for Us Who Can Be Against Us?

Think about a time in your life that others conspired against you. Describe how you felt when you were betrayed, and how you were able to forgive your betrayer.

Write a scripture that will serve as a reminder to you, for what you need to do when you are betrayed or persecuted by others.

Pray

Today as you pray with your prayer pal regarding your prayer needs, take time to pray for those people that use you, persecute you, hate you, are envious of you or make life difficult for you. Discuss your prayer journal entry with your prayer pal.

○ Prayer 1
○ Prayer 2
○ Prayer 3

Day 6: Stay in Routine and Keep on Praying!

Scripture

Now when Daniel learned that the decree had been published, he went home to his upstairs room where the windows opened toward Jerusalem. Three times a day he got down on his knees and prayed, giving thanks to his God, just as he had done before.—Daniel 6:10

Reflection

Take a minute to think about how Daniel handled this situation. Even though the king of the land passed a law to pray only unto him, Daniel went to his house and resumed praying like he always did to his God. Not only did he pray but he did it openly. However, here is the most fantastic part of this passage—he gave thanks to God despite his situation! So put yourself in Daniel's shoes, would you have had the courage to do the same? Would you have been more fearful of disobeying your earthly ruler or your heavenly ruler? Would you have kept in a routine of praying three times a day and gave thanks to God? As you stay in the habit of praying with your prayer pal, three times a day, don't forget to thank God for everything including the dark days. Instead of worrying about your problems, and whether or not God is going to deliver you from them, trust God like Daniel did and stay in the routine of praying, giving thanks to God in every situation and trusting that no matter how God responds, He does know what is best for you.

Journal

Today, stay in the routine of praying and just like Daniel give thanks to God for all your blessings. Take the time to write about the things that you are thankful for in your journal today.

Optional Social Media Challenge

On your social media tell your friends that you were given the challenge to post what you are thankful for the most. List or post a pic of what it is that you're grateful for and why. Ask your friends to keep the challenge going by sharing what they are thankful for the most. Make this your hashtag: #Iamthankful.

Prayer Journal Entry 6: Stay in Routine and Keep on Praying!

Blessings List	**Why am I thankful for this blessing?**
1.	
2.	
3.	
4.	
5.	
6.	
7.	
8.	
9.	
10.	

Pray

Discuss your journal entry with your prayer pal. This challenge is a way to train yourself to pray like Daniel did, with courage, routine and thanksgiving. Be sure that as you bring "your needs" to God that you never fail to thank Him for the blessings in your life and the prayers that He answers.

○ Prayer 1
○ Prayer 2
○ Prayer 3

Day 7: Do You Trust God?

Scripture

Then these men went as a group and found Daniel praying and asking God for help.—Daniel 6:11

Reflection

We can only imagine how excited the officers were to run back and report to the King that Daniel had defied the law. They wanted nothing more than to see Daniel dead and they knew enough about Daniel to know that he would never abandon his faith. However, consider this, what if Daniel would not have prayed openly in the way that he did? What if he was worried about defying the law of his land and chose to obey it instead? Alternatively, what if Daniel would have privately prayed because he was afraid of getting caught by the King but did not want to abandon his faith? There are times in our own lives that we are tested to see if we are committed to God. We will have choices much like Daniel did to either 100% trust God, 50% trust God or not trust God at all. Which are you?

Journal

Today consider where you are in regards to your trust with God. You will answer five questions that examine areas that Christians tend to have difficulty trusting God in. Discuss with your prayer pal ways that you can grow your trust in God.

Optional Social Media Challenge

Share a scripture with your friends about trusting God. Be sure to include a statement with your scripture that lets your friends know to put their trust in God not material things, people or places. Be creative and use personal experience as a point of reference. Make this your hashtag: #InGodITrust.

Prayer Journal Entry 7: Do You Trust God?

Do You Trust God?			
Determine which areas that you need to trust God more in by answering the following questions.			
Trust Question	**100% Trust God**	**50% Trust God**	**0% Trust God**
I trust God when it comes to my finances.			
I trust God when it comes to my health.			
I trust God in my marriage. (If not married) I trust God in helping me find a spouse.			
I trust God in my career. (If not employed) I trust God will provide me with a job. (If retired or unable to work) I trust God with my day-to-activities.			
I trust God in taking care of my children's needs. (If no children) I trust that God will provide me with a child and/or I trust that God will take care of the children closest to me.			
TOTAL			

Pray

Discuss your journal entry with your prayer pal. As you continue to pray for your prayer needs, pray for one another's ability to trust God always!

○ Prayer 1
○ Prayer 2
○ Prayer 3

Day 8: Do You Allow Your Past to Define You or Refine You?

Scripture

So they went to the king and spoke to him about his royal decree: "Did you not publish a decree that during the next thirty days anyone who prays to any god or human being except to you, Your Majesty, would be thrown into the lions' den?" The king answered, "The decree stands—in accordance with the law of the Medes and Persians, which cannot be repealed." Then they said to the king, "Daniel, who is one of the exiles from Judah, pays no attention to you, Your Majesty, or to the decree you put in writing. He still prays three times a day."—Daniel 6:12–13

Reflection

When the officers ran back to the King to report that Daniel had defied the law, they pointed out three things about Daniel that made him appear to be rebellious to the king. First, they reminded the king of Daniel's past; that he was an exile from Judah. Secondly, they wanted the king to know that Daniel disregarded his orders to worship only him. Lastly, they pointed out that not only was Daniel disregarding the king's orders, but Daniel was continuing to pray not once a day, not twice, but three times a day to his God. Now it is important to note that Daniel was never ashamed of being an exile. Daniel used this misfortune not to define him but as a way to bring glory to God. Throughout Daniel's 70 years in exile, he chose to obey God, and as a result, he quickly got the attention and respect from the kings he served. Yes, Daniel was different because he was not from Babylon, but he did not let that fact define who he was through Christ! Much like Daniel, God has created each of us for a purpose, and sometimes God will use the most unlikely people to do the most amazing things!

Journal

It is important to remember that our past should not define who we are but rather, through the help of Christ–refine us or make us better. Today in your journal, list anything from your past that you have allowed to define you. Afterward, think of how you could use your past for God's glory.

Prayer Journal Entry 8: Do You Allow Your Past to Define You or Refine You?

Describe anything from your past that you have allowed to define you.

How could you use your past for God's glory?

Pray
Today as you continue to pray for your prayer needs, take time to pray for God to help you use your past for His glory.

○ Prayer 1
○ Prayer 2
○ Prayer 3

Day 9: Are You Faced with a Decision?

Scripture

When the king heard this, he was greatly distressed; he was determined to rescue Daniel and made every effort until sundown to save Him.—Daniel 6:14

Reflection

King Darius had to make a decision–was he going to carry out the consequences of his law or was he going to amend it for his friend, Daniel? Making a decision is tricky sometimes. From the easiest of decisions like, "what should I eat?" to the more difficult ones, "should I stay in this marriage?" Maybe you are praying for God to help you decide something and it weighs heavy on your heart as to what the right thing is to do. Everything looks bleak, and you are praying for a way out. What should you do?

Journal

It is always important to use wisdom and pray for direction when making a decision. Today, in your journal, you will examine questions that will guide you in the decision-making process. As you go through each question, take time to reflect on each one as it applies.

Optional Social Media Challenge

Find a picture of a time in your life where you made the right decision that was guided by God. Maybe it was a job change, the day you were married, or a move you made. Post the picture on your social media and talk about how God guided you in making this decision. Make this your hashtag: #God'shelpIneveryDecision.

Prayer Journal Entry 9: Are You Faced with a Decision?

Evaluate your decision, by asking yourself the following questions:

1. Does this decision involve anything that would be contradictory to God's Holy Word?

2. Does this decision involve anything that would cause another person to fall out of the will of God?

3. Does this decision involve secrets or anything that I would be ashamed of others knowing?

4. If someone else were making this decision what would you tell them to do?

5. Will this decision hinder my growth in Christ or take time away from me serving Him?

6. Will this decision bring honor to God in some way?

7. Have I prayed or asked others to pray for me about this decision?

Pray
As you and your prayer pal pray about any decisions that you have to make, ask God for wisdom in helping you make the best decision. Share your journal entry with your prayer pal and take time to pray that God will direct you to the right choice.

○ Prayer 1
○ Prayer 2
○ Prayer 3

Day 10: Is Your Fate Sealed?

Scripture

Then the men went as a group to King Darius and said to him, "Remember, Your Majesty, that according to the law of the Medes and Persians no decree or edict that the king issues can be changed." So the king gave the order, and they brought Daniel and threw him into the lions' den. The king said to Daniel, "May your God, whom you serve continually, rescue you!"—Daniel 6:15–16

Reflection

Are you at a point in your life where you feel that your fate is sealed? Maybe you have been given a health diagnosis that it is impossible to cure, or made a decision that you regret, or sinned and think there is no turning back. Look at Daniel in these scriptures—Man's fate for him was sealed—he should have been a dead man—but God's fate for Daniel wasn't sealed—God had a plan. No matter what man says, God always takes care of His children! Be strong like Daniel today, remember to trust God in the situations that are hopeless.

Journal

Today in your journal, you will once again evaluate your mind, body, and spirit since you began this challenge. Think about how your thoughts are changing, think about what you are doing for the Lord, and think about how your spirit is connecting with Christ. (This entry will be shared with your prayer pal or your prayer pal group so be sure to self-reflect and consider how you have grown as a prayer warrior).

Optional Social Media Challenge

Take time to post on your social media how Prayer Pals 21-Day Challenge is changing your life. Be sure to link your friends to Prayer Pals 21-Day Challenge on Facebook so that they can learn more about the challenge. Make this your hashtag: #PrayerPals21DayChallengeisChangingme.

Prayer Journal Entry 10: Mind, Body, and Spirit Mid-Point Questionnaire

Mind

Do you read your bible daily?	Yes	No
Do you spend time talking to God each day?	Yes	No
Do you meditate on the scripture each day?	Yes	No
Do you worry, fear or doubt about things in your life?	Yes	No

Body

Do you use your talents to serve God in some way?	Yes	No
Do you witness the gospel to others each day?	Yes	No
Do you praise God throughout your day?	Yes	No
Do you present your body as a living sacrifice for Christ?	Yes	No

Spirit

Do you feel close to God?	Yes	No
Do you keep the commandments?	Yes	No

After you complete the mid-point, Mind, Body, and Spirit Questionnaire, you will compare your answers to the initial one that was completed on day 1. Is there any area(s) of growth? Discuss below.

Pray

Congratulations! You are at the mid-point of your challenge today. Share with your pal how you have gotten stronger during the prayer challenge.

- ○ Prayer 1
- ○ Prayer 2
- ○ Prayer 3

Day 11: When There is no Hope!

Scripture

A stone was brought and placed over the mouth of the den, and the king sealed it with his own signet ring and with the rings of his nobles, so that Daniel's situation might not be changed.—Daniel 6:17

Reflection

Daniel's situation appeared to be hopeless. Sometimes we are faced with situations that are much like Daniels' where we feel alone and defeated. Maybe, it's a doctor's words saying he or she can do no more for you, or perhaps it is relationship problems, or financial problems, infertility issues, job loss, or even church problems. Above all, God needs you to not look at your problem through man's eyes but rather through His eyes!

Journal

Today is your day to self-reflect. Everything you know about God and the way He has taken care of you should be thought about today. From the day He saved you, to a day He healed you, to a time that He carried you through a painful situation, to a day that He delivered you from something impossible. After you have reflected about the things God has already delivered you from, take time to write about them in your journal. This entry will serve as your reminder throughout the remainder of this challenge, to trust God and have hope, because a deliverance from God is coming!

Optional Social Media Challenge

Share one thing that you wrote about in your journal today with your friends on social media. #myGodprovides

Prayer Journal Entry 11: When There is no Hope!

Describe the day you gave your life to Christ.

Describe a time you were healed.

Describe a time you were carried through a painful situation.

Describe a time when you were delivered from a problem.

Pray
Today as you pray with your prayer pal, take a few minutes to share with them your journal entry. Pray with a boldness that God is going to deliver you once again!

                                                 ○ Prayer 1
                                                 ○ Prayer 2
                                                 ○ Prayer 3

Day 12: God Is Working on Your Behalf!

Scripture

Then the king returned to his palace and spent the night without eating and without any entertainment being brought to him. And he could not sleep.—Daniel 6:18

Reflection

The Bible does not give an account as to what was going on inside the lion's den the night that Daniel was in it. However, it does give an account of what the man who was responsible for carrying out the consequence was doing. These scriptures indicate that King Darius could not eat, could not sleep and did not desire any entertainment. Is there something to be learned or proven through this story? One would naturally think that the drama in this story would be with the person in the lion's den rather than the person sitting comfortably in a King's castle, right? However, the reality of the story was that while Daniel was at ease in the lion's den, God was working on his behalf, opening the hearts and eyes of the people around Daniel. So what does this mean? God does the same for us! While we are in "the lion's den" we should keep our eyes on God, pray and let Him fight our battle. That is how "trust" is built.

Journal

Today as you pray with your partner, encourage each other to trust God like Daniel did because God is working on your behalf. Write down your favorite scripture about "trust" in your journal today, and share it with your prayer partner today. Reflect about a time when God worked something out behind the scenes for you.

Optional Social Media Challenge

Post the scripture you have chosen on social media so that your friends can see it too! Make this your hashtag: #GodisWorkingonMybehalf.

Prayer Journal Entry 12: God is Working on Your Behalf

My "trust" scripture is:

"I trust God because....."

"A time in my life when God worked something out on my behalf was............."

Pray

As God is working on your behalf, remember to trust Him in all situations even when it looks bleak. Although you may be in a situation that appears hopeless, God always provides! Today, as you pray, have confidence that God is working the details out while you are waiting. Thank Him in your prayers today with your prayer pal!

                  ○ Prayer 1
                  ○ Prayer 2
                  ○ Prayer 3

Day 13: Is Your Trial Allowing Others to See Your Faith?

Scripture

At the first light of dawn, the king got up and hurried to the lions' den.—Daniel 6:19

Reflection

King Darius' sleep was gone, so when morning came he could not wait to run to the lion's den to see if Daniel's God had delivered him! As you think about Daniel's circumstance and the King's eagerness to see if Daniel's God delivered, consider this question: Was Daniel's trial for him to learn or grow from, or was Daniel's trial for the King and the people around him? Sometimes as Christians, we go through things that ultimately build our faith, but sometimes we go through things so that others can see our faith. One can only imagine the audience that was watching and waiting to see if Daniel's God would prevail. In the world we live in today, people are always watching you as a Christian, and waiting to see if the God you serve is real. We all desire deliverance out of our problems, but stay strong like Daniel, remember there is an audience watching, and wait patiently on your rescue–because it's coming!

Journal

In your journal, you will write down one of your prayers and consider whether or not God is using this prayer as a way to grow you spiritually, or as a way to demonstrate the power of Christ to someone else or both.

Example:

Prayer Need: I have been praying for the last three years for a job change—and I am still waiting for God to answer it.

How could God be growing you spiritually through this? I think God is teaching me to be patient and to trust Him. I tend to want to try to fix my problems but when I do they always backfire. I must learn to "let go" and trust God!

How might God use your prayer need as a way to reach others: God may be leaving me in this job as a way to witness to my co-workers.

Journal Entry 13: Is Your Trial Allowing Others to See Your Faith?

My Prayer Need Is:

How might God be growing you spiritually through this?

How might God use your prayer need as a way to reach others?

Pray

Today as you pray with your pal, discuss your journal entry with them, and take time to thank God for how He is using your trial for His Glory!

○ Prayer 1
○ Prayer 2
○ Prayer 3

Day 14: Will Others Notice?

Scripture

When he came near the den, he called to Daniel in an anguished voice, "Daniel, servant of the living God, has your God, whom you serve continually, been able to rescue you from the lions?"—Daniel 6:20

Reflection

Although Daniel had been in the lion's den all night, it was King Darius who was found to be in a state of suffering. He had not eaten nor slept throughout the night, and unlike most Kings, was feeling sorrowful for his decision to throw Daniel in the lion's den. Take a minute to think about the words that King Darius spoke when he arrived at the lion's den, "Daniel, servant of the living God, has your God, whom you serve continually, been able to rescue you from the lions?" Here is the interesting part about King Darius' words: 1. He refers to Daniel as being a servant to a "living" God. Therefore, Darius acknowledges that the God Daniel served was alive and active. 2. He refers to Daniel "continually" serving his God no matter what the consequences were. Darius saw firsthand, how courageous Daniel was and that Daniel feared the consequences of his God more than him. 3. King Darius had hope that the living God that Daniel served was able to rescue him. So here is the question, "What would lead Darius to believe that Daniel's God was able to rescue him? After all, Daniel was in a den of hungry lions. As you move through your prayer challenge, people are watching you. Today consider the ways that you are making an impression on others. Are the people around you witnessing your devotion to prayer three times a day? Have they heard you talk about your prayer challenge or testify to the good things that God has been doing? Have they seen your post on social media? Are they interested in God because of the commitment you are making to pray? If so, then you are making an impression on others like the one Daniel did on King Darius.

Journal

Today, consider how your commitment to this prayer challenge has gotten the attention of the people around you. Have others witnessed you praying, working on your challenge book, or responded to your social media posts? In your journal, write about how you are influencing others during your prayer challenge.

Prayer Journal Entry 14: Will Others Notice?

Have others witnessed you praying? Reflect about who and why this may be important.

Have others witnessed you working on your challenge book? Reflect about who and why this may be important.

Have others responded to your social media posts? If so, which social media posts seem to be the most effective?

Consider how your commitment to this prayer challenge has gotten the attention of the people around you.

Pray

Today as you and your prayer pal join together and pray, ask God to help you be more like Him so that whenever others see your good works, they will see Christ through you.

○ Prayer 1
○ Prayer 2
○ Prayer 3

Day 15: An Eye for an Eye, A Tooth for a Tooth, Right?

Scripture

Daniel answered, "May the king live forever!—Daniel 6:21

Reflection

After King, Darius called out to Daniel to confirm whether or not he was alive; Daniel spoke these compelling words to the man who sentenced him to death, "May the king live forever!" This phrase was generally spoken to kings throughout history as an expression of respect and honor. So why is this important? Rather than Daniel expressing hatred, disregard or resentment towards the king for sentencing him to death, Daniel conveyed that he still valued the King for who he was and forgave him of his actions. When we are betrayed, persecuted or let down by someone we should not render back the same treatment; like the old saying, an eye for an eye, a tooth for a tooth. Instead, we should handle it with kindness and forgiveness just like Daniel did. Today take time to reflect about this question, if you were in Daniel's situation, would you have forgiven the King for throwing you in the lion's den or would you have been angry or upset at him and hoping that God would punish Him in some way?

Journal

Daniel exemplified the kind of servant that we should model ourselves after. In your journal today, think about the one thing that you would have difficulty forgiving or a type of person that you would have trouble showing love and kindness to. After you have identified the "thing" or the "person" that is difficult to forgive or show love and kindness to, think about ways that God has forgiven you, and taught you grace and mercy. Are you any different than King Darius? Discuss your answer in your journal today.

Optional Social Media Challenge

Kindness is something that the world needs to see more! Today it is your opportunity to perform an act of kindness on social media.

Prayer Journal Entry 15: An Eye for an Eye, a Tooth for a Tooth, Right?

What are some things or types of people that you have difficulty forgiving?

In what ways has God forgiven you and why is it important to extend that mercy to others?

How willing would you have been to forgive King Darius if you were in Daniel's shoes? Would you have shown him the same amount of respect and kindness as Daniel?

Pray
Today as you pray with your pal about your needs, ask God to give you a heart like Daniel to forgive others.

○ Prayer 1
○ Prayer 2
○ Prayer 3

Day 16: A Test and then a Testimony?

Scripture

My God sent his angel, and he shut the mouths of the lions. They have not hurt me, because I was found innocent in his sight. Nor have I ever done any wrong before you, Your Majesty."—Daniel 6:22

Reflection

Daniel had endured a night in the lion's den but how? I am sure that this was the burning question on the King's mind as well others that were present witnessing this miracle. However, Daniel did not waste any time; it was his opportunity to share his testimony and let everyone know that his God had delivered him from the lions! Sometimes when our deliverance comes, we forget to do the most important thing, share our testimony. Today as you are winding up the last week of your prayer challenge be willing to share your testimony!

Journal

In your journal today, practice writing down a testimony you have. Note: Sometimes testimonies can be painful to share because they often bring up painful memories that you want to forget. However, here is a little rhyme to remind you of why your testimony should be shared: "If you don't share your story, then God doesn't get His glory!"

Optional Social Media Challenge

If you want to take your testimony to the next level, share it with your friends on social media. Make this your Hashtag: #ThisisMytestimony.

Prayer Journal Entry 16: A Test and then a Testimony?

My Testimony

_____
_____
_____
_____
_____
_____
_____
_____
_____
_____
_____
_____
_____
_____
_____
_____
_____
_____
_____
_____
_____
_____

Pray
Today as you pray with your prayer pal, take time to pray for courage to give your testimony. Continue to pray for your prayer needs.

○ Prayer 1
○ Prayer 2
○ Prayer 3

Day 17: A Test, a Testimony, and Then What?

Scripture

The king was overjoyed and gave orders to lift Daniel out of the den. And when Daniel was lifted from the den, no wound was found on him, because he had trusted in his God.—Daniel 6:23

Reflection

The scripture indicates that the King was overjoyed to witness Daniel's deliverance. One can only imagine how much relief that the King felt after seeing Daniel safe and unharmed! It is evident that this miracle left a lasting impression on King Darius because he had encountered God through Daniel. Daniel's story did not end at the lion's den-instead Daniel's story brings about God's glory as King Darius' later commands his entire kingdom to worship the God of Daniel.

Journal

After God answers your prayers and you share testimony with others, what should you do next? In your journal, think about how you can expand your testimony to reach new people or how you can use your testimony to create a ministry for yourself. Maybe you were delivered from a disease that was terminal or given a child that the doctors said you would not conceive, or given a job that you did not think was possible. Whatever the situation might be, think of how you could take your testimony and expand it to new audiences or make a ministry out of it. Write down your ideas in your journal and also allow your prayer pal to give you some input.

Optional Social Media Challenge

If you have been thinking about expanding your testimony to reach new people or creating a ministry from it, use social media as a way to connect.

Prayer Journal Entry 17: A Test, a Testimony, and Then What?

Have you ever shared your testimony? If so, to whom?

How many people would you estimate has heard your testimony?

How could you use your testimony to reach new people or how could you use your testimony to begin a ministry?

What steps will you need to take to expand your testimony?

Pray

With your prayer pal today, discuss ways to expand your testimony. Continue praying for your prayer needs and ask God to help you grow your testimony.

○ Prayer 1
○ Prayer 2
○ Prayer 3

Day 18: But What about Those Evildoers?

Scripture

At the king's command, the men who had falsely accused Daniel were brought in and thrown into the lions' den, along with their wives and children. And before they reached the floor of the den, the lions overpowered them and crushed all their bones.—Daniel 6:24

Reflection

God will take care of the evildoers in his righteous way. Don't waste your time or energy thinking, planning or conspiring against evildoers. If anything, pray for them, offer kind words to them, and love them through your actions; who knows God may be using you to reach them!

Journal

Today in your journal evaluate how you respond to evil-doers. Are you the type of person that lives by the saying what goes around comes around? Consider Daniel when he came out of the lion's den, he didn't become angry with the king for putting him in there or tell the king to put the evil doers in the lion's den. Instead, Daniel allowed the King of the Kingdom to make his judgment. So what about you? Are you a revenge-seeking person or are you like Daniel?

Optional Social Media Challenge

Today you will post scripture about love on your social media. Make this your hashtag: #GodlovesUsall.

Prayer Journal Entry 18: But What about Those Evildoers?

Think about a time in your life when you were wronged or treated badly by someone. Describe how you responded to this situation.

What you would change about the situation above if you had an opportunity to do it over again?

Pray

Take time to share out your journal entry with your prayer pal and pray with them for the evildoers of the world.

    ○ Prayer 1
    ○ Prayer 2
    ○ Prayer 3

Day 19: Celebrate God!

Scripture

Then King Darius wrote to all the nations and peoples of every language in all the earth:
"May you prosper greatly!
"I issue a decree that in every part of my kingdom people must fear and reverence the God of Daniel.
"For he is the living God
        and he endures forever;
his kingdom will not be destroyed,
        his dominion will never end.
He rescues and he saves;
        he performs signs and wonders
        in the heavens and on the earth.
He has rescued Daniel
        from the power of the lions."
—Daniel 6:25-27

Reflect

This is a time to rejoice in those prayers answered during the 21-day challenge, and tell someone about them—Just as King Darius was excited to tell his entire Kingdom about the God of Daniel!

Journal

You are almost at the end of your challenge, so it is time to start planning your Prayer Pals 21 Day Celebration! List some ideas of things in your journal that you and your prayer pal could do to celebrate completing this challenge. Ideas could range from a small gift or card exchange, a post to each other on social media or a day out to celebrate.

Optional Social Media Challenge

Invite your friends and family on social to be a part of your celebration!

Prayer Journal Entry 19: Celebrate God!

My Prayer Pals 21-Day Challenge Celebration Plans Are:

Pray

As you get closer to the end of your prayer challenge, you and your prayer pal take time to celebrate God and give Him Praise during your prayers today for all he has done!

    ○ Prayer 1
    ○ Prayer 2
    ○ Prayer 3

Day 20: Blessings From God!

Scripture

So Daniel prospered during the reign of Darius and the reign of Cyrus the Persian.—Daniel 6:28

Reflection

After Daniel was betrayed, sentenced to death, placed in a lion's den, and delivered, one last thing happened—Daniel prospered. Sometimes when we are facing our tests and trials, or feel like all hope is gone, remember to keep "pressing through," praying and believing that God can do all things. Just like Daniel, you will get to experience God's grace and mercy as He rescues you from your tests and trials!

Journal

As your 21-day challenge comes to a close, it is time to think of what you have "gained" during this journey. Maybe it is a whole new understanding of God, how to talk to Him, the importance of praying with another person, or just prayers answered. Whatever it is, use the Prayer Pals 4 essential components to evaluate your gains!

Optional Social Media Challenge

Share out the four essential components of Prayer Pals using this acrostic: (You can find it on the Prayer Pals 21-Day Challenge Facebook Page)

P represents "persistency." Think about it like this-----your prayer is brought before God 3 times a day for 21 days!

R. represents "routine" (forming a relationship with God as you pray each day three times a day). Getting into a habit of praying even when you are tired, hopeless, or feeling defeated. Praying with your pal will eventually become a natural part of your day, and you have gained a praying pal for life!

A. Represents "alliance" having a partner to share your burdens and pray with you. There is power in numbers!

Y. Represents "your needs" poured out to God. Things that have hindered you from growing, things that you gave up on praying about or any other need—give them to God and pray persistently!

Journal Entry 20: Blessings of God!

Persistency-How has persistently praying to God changed you?

Routine- How has praying every day, three times a day, changed you?

Alliance-How has praying with a pal changed you?

Your Needs-What prayers have been answered?

Pray
Take time to thank and praise God today for bringing you and your prayer pal together. Continue praying for your prayer needs because it's not over yet!

- O Prayer 1
- O Prayer 2
- O Prayer 3

Day 21: God Has Heard You from the Beginning!

Scripture

Then he continued, "Do not be afraid, Daniel. Since the first day that you set your mind to gain understanding and to humble yourself before your God, your words were heard, and I have come in response to them.—Daniel 10:12

Reflection

If you read Daniel Chapter 10 you will find that several years after Daniel was in the lion's den he faced yet another test of his faith. This time Daniel did not get the "quick response" from God, as he often had. However, after 21 days of praying, God's messenger showed up and told Daniel that God had heard him since the first prayer he had prayed. So is there a lesson to be learned from Daniel 10:12? Yes, God has heard every prayer you have prayed since the beginning (even before this challenge). Just like Daniel, from the moment that you submitted yourself to praying for something or someone, God heard your prayers. Sometimes it is a simple yes, sometimes it is a no, and sometimes it is a wait. So why does God make us wait? Sometimes it is all about timing. God can see the future, and we can't. Remember He loves us, so much so that He lines up the events of our lives like a perfect masterpiece. The next possibility is that sometimes God allows things to happen because he is teaching us something and is growing us. If you feel that God is silent, then reexamine what you are praying for and examine whether or not there might be something underlying that He is trying to teach you! Keep on praying and trusting God in all things, and soon an answer will come, just like it did with Daniel.

Journal

Congratulations! You have completed the 21-Day Prayer Pal Challenge. Today in your journal you will do your final evaluation of your mind, body, and spirit.

Social Media Challenge

Post Daniel 10:12 on your social media. Make this your hashtag: GodhasHeardmeFromtheBeginning.

Prayer Journal Entry 21: Mind, Body, and Spirit Final Questionnaire

Mind

Do you read your bible daily?	Yes	No
Do you spend time talking to God each day?	Yes	No
Do you meditate on the scripture each day?	Yes	No
Do you worry, fear or doubt about things in your life?	Yes	No

Body

Do you use your talents to serve God in some way?	Yes	No
Do you witness the gospel to others each day?	Yes	No
Do you praise God throughout your day?	Yes	No
Do you present your body as a living sacrifice for Christ?	Yes	No

Spirit

Do you feel close to God?	Yes	No
Do you keep the commandments?	Yes	No

After you complete the Final Mind, Body, and Spirit Questionnaire, discuss below how you have changed since beginning this challenge.

Pray

Today you and your prayer pal will reflect on your last 21 days and compare how your mind, body, and spirit have changed throughout this challenge. You will also take time to celebrate and give God praise!

○ Prayer 1
○ Prayer 2
○ Prayer 3

Prayer Pals 21-Day Challenge

POST-CHALLENGE

Prayer Pals 21-Day Post Challenge

Next Steps

Congratulations on completing your Prayer Pals 21-Day Challenge!
Now, what is the next step?

- Prayer Pals 21 wants to reward you for completing the 21-Day Challenge. On page 117, you will find your Prayer Pals 21-day challenge completion certificate. Please complete the following steps to conclude your challenge:

  1. Fill in your first and last name on your certificate.

  2. Remove Certificate from the booklet.

  3. Take a picture of you and your prayer pal holding your certificates and post it on your social media using the hashtag: #prayerpals21daychallengecomplete. (If you are unable to take a picture with your pal, post a picture of just yourself holding your certificate.

  ★★★If you are completing this challenge as a group, your Prayer Pals 21-day leader, will be presenting your certificate at the celebration ceremony.

- Sometimes Prayer Pals want to continue praying or change partners after they have completed the 21-Day Challenge. If you are still being directed to keep on praying with your prayer pal or to change partners, then don't stop! If you want to keep praying with your pal, check out the Prayer Pals Continuation Journal beginning on Page 73 that will give you 21 more days to pray with your pal. If you want to start this challenge with a different pal, then you and your pal will need a new 21-Day Challenge Book.

- If you are interested in sharing this challenge with others, Prayer Pals 21 would like to invite you to become a leader of this ministry. As a leader, you will have the exciting opportunity to form a group of "praying pals" at your church or organization and conduct a 21-Day Challenge. If you are interested in becoming a Prayer Pals 21 Leader, read the Prayer Pals 21-Day Challenge Leader steps found on page 72.

Prayer Pals 21-Day Challenge Leader Steps

Step 1	Step 2	Step 3
Get Permission	**Organize Your Informational Meeting**	**Initiate Your Informational Meeting**
To complete a 21-day challenge at your church or organization obtain the permission and support of your pastor or leader. Be sure to share with Pastor or leader Prayer Pals 21-Day Challenge 4 essential principles found on page 21.	Select a date, time and location for your 21-Day Challenge Informational Meeting Give potential challengers at least a week or more notice about the meeting. Use the Prayer Pals 21-Day Challenge flyer as a way to invite others to the challenge found on Facebook page.	The leader will explain the purpose of Prayer Pals 21-Day Challenge using the Acrostic-PRAY. The leader will walk potential challengers through the Pre-challenge stage. The leader will set a date for challengers to begin. It is encouraged that leaders set a celebration date after 21 days.
Step 4	Step 5	Step 6
Stay Connected	**Mid-Point Meeting**	**Celebration of Challenge**
Once challenge begins, it is crucial that you stay connected with your challenge members. An excellent way to do that is by creating a private group on social media. If you decide not to create a private group on social media, it is strongly encouraged that you meet at mid-point with your challenge members.	At mid-point (after day 10) you have the option to meet with members in person to pray as a group.	At the end of 21 days, you will celebrate your group's completion of the 21-day prayer pal challenge. Be sure to hand out certificates of completion during the celebration. Some groups have celebration of 21-Day Challenge ceremonies.

Prayer Pals 21-Day Challenge

CONTINUATION JOURNAL

Prayer Journal Entry 22

Scripture

Let us then approach God's throne of grace with confidence, so that we may receive mercy and find grace to help us in our time of need.—Hebrews 4:16

Journal

How do you approach God's throne? Are you doubtful or fearful or are you fully confident that God is listening to your petitions? Take time to self-reflect about the confidence that you have in Christ.

_____

_____

_____

_____

_____

_____

_____

_____

_____

_____

_____

_____

_____

_____

_____

_____

_____

_____

_____

_____

_____

_____

Prayer Journal Entry 23

Scripture

Ask and it will be given to you; seek and you will find; knock and the door will be opened to you. For everyone who asks receives; the one who seeks finds; and to the one who knocks, the door will be opened.—Matthew 7:7–8

Journal

In your journal today, write a letter to God asking Him to open up the door to your prayer needs.

Prayer Journal Entry 24

Scripture

Give thanks to the God of heaven. His love endures forever.—Psalm 136:26

Journal

In today's journal entry, write a letter to God thanking Him for all your blessings.

_____

_____

_____

_____

_____

_____

_____

_____

_____

_____

_____

_____

_____

_____

_____

_____

_____

_____

_____

_____

_____

_____

Prayer Journal Entry 25

Scripture

But when you ask, you must believe and not doubt, because the one who doubts is like a wave of the sea, blown and tossed by the wind.—James 1:6

Journal

Describe a past experience where you doubted God. What happened as a result of your doubt?

_____

_____

_____

_____

_____

_____

_____

_____

_____

_____

_____

_____

_____

_____

_____

_____

_____

_____

_____

_____

_____

_____

_____

Prayer Journal Entry 26

Scripture

Be joyful in hope, patient in affliction, and faithful in prayer.—Romans 12:12

Journal

Describe a time that you were patient in affliction and faithful in prayer.

_____

_____

_____

_____

_____

_____

_____

_____

_____

_____

_____

_____

_____

_____

_____

_____

_____

_____

_____

_____

_____

_____

_____

_____

_____

Prayer Journal Entry 27

Memory Verse

Rejoice always, pray continually, give thanks in all circumstances; for this is God's will for you in Christ Jesus.—1 Thessalonians 5:16-18

Journal

In today's journal you will self-reflect. Ask yourself these questions, do you rejoice in the Lord each day, pray continually and give thanks to God in all circumstances?

_____

_____

_____

_____

_____

_____

_____

_____

_____

_____

_____

_____

_____

_____

_____

_____

_____

_____

_____

_____

_____

_____

Prayer Journal Entry 28

Memory Verse

Devote yourselves to prayer, being watchful and thankful.—Colossians 4:2

Journal

How has your prayer life changed? Do you find yourself more devoted to your prayers and have a heart of thankfulness?

_____

_____

_____

_____

_____

_____

_____

_____

_____

_____

_____

_____

_____

_____

_____

_____

_____

_____

_____

_____

_____

_____

_____

_____

Prayer Journal Entry 29

Scripture

In the same way, the Spirit helps us in our weakness. We do not know what we ought to pray for, but the Spirit Himself intercedes for us through wordless groans.—Romans 8:26

Journal

Write down your prayer needs. After you have wrote them down, present them to your heavenly father.

_____

_____

_____

_____

_____

_____

_____

_____

_____

_____

_____

_____

_____

_____

_____

_____

_____

_____

_____

_____

_____

_____

_____

Prayer Journal Entry 30

Scripture

In the morning, Lord, you hear my voice; in the morning I lay my requests before you and wait expectantly.—Psalm 5:3

Journal

Before you begin your day, write a prayer to God for a blessing on your day.

_____

_____

_____

_____

_____

_____

_____

_____

_____

_____

_____

_____

_____

_____

_____

_____

_____

_____

_____

_____

_____

_____

_____

_____

_____

_____

_____

_____

_____

Prayer Journal Entry 31

Scripture

Even youths grow tired and weary, and young men stumble and fall; but those who hope in the LORD will renew their strength. They will soar on wings like eagles; they will run and not grow weary, they will walk and not be faint.—Isaiah 30:40-41

Journal

Are you tired and weary today? What are the "hopes" in the Lord you have that sustain you each day?

_____

_____

_____

_____

_____

_____

_____

_____

_____

_____

_____

_____

_____

_____

_____

_____

_____

_____

_____

_____

_____

_____

Prayer Journal Entry 32

Scripture

Jesus looked at them and said, "With man this is impossible, but with God all things are possible."—Matthew 19:26

Journal

List some stories from the Bible where God was able to do the impossible, and then discuss this question, "Is anything too difficult for God?"

_____

_____

_____

_____

_____

_____

_____

_____

_____

_____

_____

_____

_____

_____

_____

_____

_____

_____

_____

_____

_____

_____

Prayer Journal Entry 33

Scripture

Answer me when I call to you, my righteous God. Give me relief from my distress; have mercy on me and hear my prayer.—Psalm 4:1

Journal

Are you desperate to hear from God today? Pour out your heart to Him today in your journal.

_____

_____

_____

_____

_____

_____

_____

_____

_____

_____

_____

_____

_____

_____

_____

_____

_____

_____

_____

_____

_____

_____

_____

Prayer Journal Entry 34

Scripture

Blessed is she who has believed that the Lord would fulfill his promises to her!—Luke 1:45

Journal

Make a list of all the strong women of faith you know, and why they are strong to you. Select one to reach out to and thank for being a strong woman of faith in your life.

_____

_____

_____

_____

_____

_____

_____

_____

_____

_____

_____

_____

_____

_____

_____

_____

_____

_____

_____

_____

_____

_____

_____

_____

Prayer Journal Entry 35

Scripture

May the God of hope fill you with all joy and peace as you trust in Him, so that you may overflow with hope by the power of the Holy Spirit.—Romans 15:13

Journal

Describe the joy and peace you have in Christ.

_____

_____

_____

_____

_____

_____

_____

_____

_____

_____

_____

_____

_____

_____

_____

_____

_____

_____

_____

_____

_____

_____

_____

_____

_____

_____

Prayer Journal Entry 36

Scripture

Trust in the LORD with all your heart and lean not on your own understanding; in all your ways submit to Him, and he will make your paths straight.—Proverbs 3:5-6

Journal

Examine your Christian walk. Are you trusting God? Are you submitting to Christ and leaning not on your own understanding?

_____

_____

_____

_____

_____

_____

_____

_____

_____

_____

_____

_____

_____

_____

_____

_____

_____

_____

_____

_____

_____

_____

Prayer Journal Entry 37

Scripture

Finally, brothers and sisters, whatever is true, whatever is noble, whatever is right, whatever is pure, whatever is lovely, whatever is admirable—if anything is excellent or praiseworthy—think about such things.—Philippians 4:8

Journal

Today, take time to reflect on the things that you are occupying your mind with and investing your energy in. Are they things which are pleasing to God?

_____

_____

_____

_____

_____

_____

_____

_____

_____

_____

_____

_____

_____

_____

_____

_____

_____

_____

_____

_____

_____

_____

_____

_____

Prayer Journal Entry 38

Scripture

He replied, "Because you have so little faith. Truly I tell you, if you have faith as small as a mustard seed, you can say to this mountain, 'Move from here to there,' and it will move. Nothing will be impossible for you." Matthew 17:20

Journal

Rejoice, knowing that all things are possible with God. Write a prayer of praise to Him today. Begin your journal by saying: "I praise you God because…."

_____

_____

_____

_____

_____

_____

_____

_____

_____

_____

_____

_____

_____

_____

_____

_____

_____

_____

_____

_____

_____

Prayer Journal Entry 39

Scripture

The LORD is my rock, my fortress and my deliverer; my God is my rock, in whom I take refuge, my shield and the horn of my salvation, my stronghold.—Psalm 18:2

Journal

How has the Lord been your rock, fortress, deliverer, refuge, shield, and stronghold?

_____

_____

_____

_____

_____

_____

_____

_____

_____

_____

_____

_____

_____

_____

_____

_____

_____

_____

_____

_____

_____

_____

Prayer Journal Entry 40

Scripture

Have I not commanded you? Be strong and courageous. Do not be afraid; do not be discouraged, for the LORD your God will be with you wherever you go.—Joshua 1:9

Journal

How have I grown stronger in Christ?

_____

_____

_____

_____

_____

_____

_____

_____

_____

_____

_____

_____

_____

_____

_____

_____

_____

_____

_____

_____

_____

_____

Prayer Journal Entry 41

Scripture

For I know the plans I have for you," declares the LORD, "plans to prosper you and not to harm you, plans to give you hope and a future.—Jeremiah 29:11

Journal

Describe any spiritual goals that you have. What must you do to achieve your spiritual goals?

_____

_____

_____

_____

_____

_____

_____

_____

_____

_____

_____

_____

_____

_____

_____

_____

_____

_____

_____

_____

_____

_____

_____

Prayer Journal Entry 42

Scripture

Be very careful, then, how you live—not as unwise but as wise, making the most of every opportunity, because the days are evil.—Ephesians 5:15-16

Journal

If you knew you only had a short time to live, what would you do differently? What is keeping you from doing these things now?

_____

_____

_____

_____

_____

_____

_____

_____

_____

_____

_____

_____

_____

_____

_____

_____

_____

_____

_____

_____

_____

_____

Certificate of Completion
Prayer Pals
21-Day Challenge

This Certifies That:

_____

Name

Successfully completed the 21 Day Prayer Pal Challenge with:

_____

Prayer Pal's Name

Presented By:

Kristin Overstreet

Prayer Pals 21-Day Challenge Program Creator

About the Author

Kristin Overstreet received a B.A. in Counseling and Human Services and a M.ed. in Mental Health Counseling from Lindsey Wilson College. She also received a MAT in Secondary Social Studies from the University of the Cumberlands. She is currently a high school history teacher at East Ridge High School in Eastern, KY, and an Adjunct Instructor for Lindsey Wilson College's School of Professional Counseling.

Prior to teaching, Kristin was a Clinical Social Worker for the state of Kentucky, where her role was to protect the needs of abused and neglected children, as well as approve and certify foster/ adoptive parents. Kristin accredits her deep relationship with Christ to the struggles and pain she faced while working in the field of Social Work.

In 2014, Kristin Overstreet received the Excellence in Service Award from the Commissioner of Kentucky, for her dedication to families and children.

Kristin is married to her husband, Lee, and the couple has 3 children, Jacob (18), Hannah (14) and Jaron (7). The family resides in Elkhorn City, KY where they are active members at Elkhorn Community Church; leading various ministries including worship music and youth ministries. Kristin also leads a women's ministry known as Faith, Family and Friends and holds two women conferences a year for women in her community.

Printed in the United States
By Bookmasters